ABOUT THE AUT

Sue D..._, known for his world-renow... *Five-Star* travel series, including *The Five-Star Guide to Airports*, *The Five-Star Guide to Hospitals*, *The Five-Star Guide to Oceans*, and *The Five-Star Guide to Waco*.

May Dupp is a national cartoonist whose daily strips, Lieutenant Dog and Stupid School, are distributed in print newspapers through King Features Syndicate.

ABOUT THE ILLUSTRATOR

Faye Kname is the best-selling author of *U: A Letter to You,* a self-help journey to find inner peace through simple alphabetic exercises, and *Blind Executive*, an epic international political thriller about a conspiracy to defraud the first visually-impaired President.

WEDDINGS
ARE A JOKE!

*THE **123 BEST JOKES** ABOUT MARRIAGE,*
GETTING MARRIED, AND BEING MARITAL

written by
Sue D. Nymm & Faye Kname

illustrations by
May Dupp

___ are a Joke
Brooklyn, NY
www.areajoke.com
2018

Weddings are a Joke!
The 123 Best Jokes About Marriage, Getting Married, and Being Marital

Copyright © 2018 by Kristi Forsch and Greg Ott
Illustrations copyright © 2018 Ed Witt

All rights reserved. This book or any portion thereof may not be reproduced or used in any manner whatsoever without the express written permission of the publisher except for the use of brief quotations in a book review or scholarly journal.

First Printing: 2018
ISBN: 9781731210074

___ are a Joke
Brooklyn, NY
www.areajoke.com

This book is dedicated to approximately 140 of our closest friends and family.

What did the jalapeño and the green pepper do for their first dance?

Salsa.

Where did the bees go after the wedding?
The honeymoon

Did you hear about the haberdashers who were most excited about getting dressed before their ceremony?
They couldn't wait to knot the tie.

Why didn't the marriage between the mouse and trackpad work out?
They were cursored.

Why was the mustard so touched by her mother-in-law's speech?
She was paid some lovely condiments.

How did the condensation upon the blades of grass receive one another's vows?
"I dew."

Why did the groom call the bride's phone during the ceremony?
To give her a wedding ring.

Did you hear about the two pilots who had a really boring wedding?
It was kind of plane.

How did the two corpses conclude their vows?
"'Til life do us part."

Where did the roofing contractors fall in love?
A shingles cruise.

How did the pies know they were right for each other?
They just had a good filling.

Where did the pens insist on getting married?
A fountain.

Did you hear about the two scientists who were wed aboard the International Space Station?

They tied the astronaut.

Where did Christmas take Thanksgiving for their honeymoon?
The Holiday Inn.

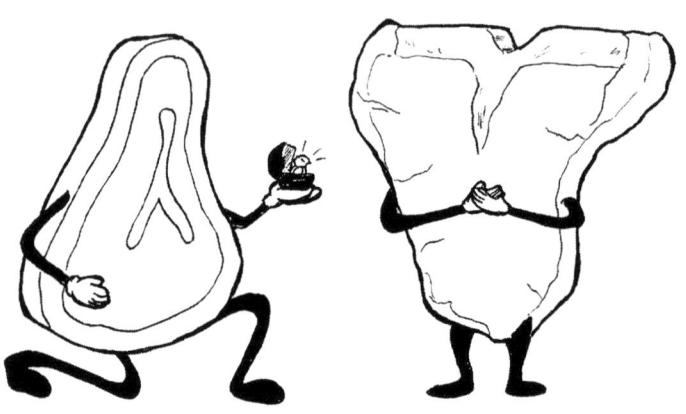

How did the pork chop propose to the steak?
"Will you marry meat?"

How did the deer exchange their vows?
"I doe."

Why was the officiant sure the monkeys were going to have a wonderful marriage?
They were bananas for each other.

What did the pine tree promise the oak?
"I'll never leave you."

What did the mathematicians serve their guests for dessert?
Pi.

Why did the cell phones have such a lousy wedding?
The poor reception.

Did you hear about how much the hot dogs enjoyed their ceremony?
They relished the moment.

Why didn't the condiments put a wedding announcement in the paper?
They figured you mustaheard.

What did the Corona Light say when his daughter told her that she was marrying her longtime partner?
"It's about lime."

What did the corn say in their vows?
"I'll love you for ears to come."

Did you hear about the members of the National Rifle Association who decided to get married?

They're having a shotgun wedding.

Did you hear about the salad who looked absolutely stunning during her wedding?

She found the perfect dressing.

Did you hear about the beds that got together?

They were wed in Holy Mattressmony.

Why did the blood get married?
They were each other's type.

How did the grape propose to their love?
"Will you be vine?"

What food did the phalanges serve their guests?
Finger foods.

And the podiatrists?
Toma-toes.

Why did Sara Lee make such a great maid of honor?
Her toast.

Why did the patient fall for the ophthalmologist?
It was love at first sight.

Why did the bibliographer fall for the librarian?
It was love at first cite.

Why did the URL fall for the web browser?
It was love at first site.

Why did the groom perform the Heimlich maneuver on his aunt during the ceremony?
She was getting all choked up.

Why were the library books wed?
It was overdue.

Why was the mouse such a great photographer?
They got everyone to say cheese.

Why didn't the letters have a wedding ceremony?
They chose to envelope.

Why was the groom so disappointed with how his bride looked at the nudist colony?

She said yes to the dress.

Did you hear about the Catan players who got married?
They settled for each other.

What was the Pillsbury Dough Boy's daughter up to at the wedding?
She was the flour girl.

Where did the groom win his fiancee's knockoff diamond ring in a game of chance and skill?
Cubic Zirconey Island.

Have you heard about the two clouds that are strongly considering marriage?
They're very cirrus.

What was the grizzly's role in the wedding party?
The ring bear.

Did you hear about the farmer who thought he'd get stood up?
He was afraid she might bale.

Whose memories did the pigeons celebrate during their ceremony?
Their late feathers.

What kind of wedding cake did the baseball players get?
A bunt.

What did the poker players serve during their cocktail hour?
Chips.

WEDDINGS ARE A JOKE!

Did you hear about the prisoners' wedding where they torched a bunch of mattresses, raided the commissary, kidnapped a couple of guards, and beat the warden to death?

It was a riot.

What do you call a bad husband?
O.J. Simpson.

Did you hear about the middle-aged tennis professionals who finally got married?
They were 40-love.

For what length of time did the wolves pledge their love to one another?
Howl their lives.

What was the blackjack dealer's one stipulation before marrying the player?
She had to be 21.

Why was the blind man so smitten by his bride?
She was the most beautiful woman he never laid eyes on.

Why did the dyslexic seem so apprehensive about marrying his bride?
He said, "Do I?"

What did the almond farmers sign before the wedding?
A pre-nut.

Did you hear about the construction supervisor who attended his mohel's wedding, had too much wine, and stopped being served by the bartenders?
They cut off the foreman.

Did you hear that Dr. Brown invited hundreds of sodas to his wedding?
It was a a huge Cel-Ray-bration.

How did the priest kick off the football players' nuptials?
"Please be CTE'd."

During the marriage of the simple machines, what did the pulley promise the inclined plane?

He'd never lever.

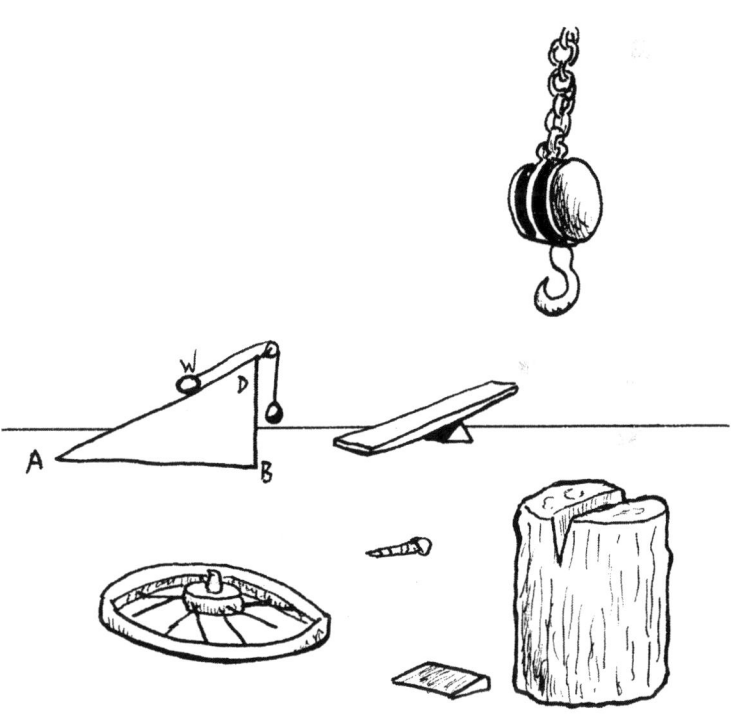

Why did the veterinarian fall in love with the construction worker?
His cat calls.

Why did the geneticists fall in love?
They were cell mates.

Did you hear about the train conductor who got alcohol poisoning at the open bar?
He drank too much cabooze.

Why did the banker finally pop the question?
He saw the benefit of a long-term investment.

What's it called when you go on a blind date during your own wedding?
An arranged marriage.

Why did everyone keep calling the bride Barbecue?
She was sauced.

Did you hear about the lightbulb who was stood up at his own wedding?
He got screwed.

How did the pirate know she was "the one?"
Her chest and booty.

When did the groom wear a dress and the bride wear a suit?
Their reversal dinner.

How did the baseball fall in love with the one who caught her?
From the moment they mitt, they were in glove.

What did the Russian groom affix to his suit lapel?

A Putinnière

How did the lumberjack propose to his husband?
"Wood you marry me?"

What did the horse say when the donkey proposed?
Neigh.

Did you hear about the janitor's best man speech?
He kept it pretty clean.

Where did the rain clouds get married?
Their wetting.

Did you hear about the homeless guys who got turned away from the wedding?
They were bummed out.

Why were the firemen excited to meet the bridesmaids?
They heard they were hose.

Did you hear about the mollusks who ran off and got married in secret?
They scalloped.

Why did the chef marry the baker?
She wanted all his bread.

Did you hear about the gardeners who crashed the wedding?
They soiled the whole affair.

Why wouldn't Hillary Clinton stop bothering the waitstaff?
She was trying to find a missing server.

Even though the nuns knew they would never be allowed to get married, what kind of reception did they dream about throwing?
A long celibation.

Where were the serial killers registered for gifts?

John Wayne Macy's.

Why did the bride and groom get married in a CompUSA?

They got a great Dell.

What did the cat insist upon before getting married?

Signing a pre-nip.

How did the salmon feed their guests?
Their wedding was capered.

Why did the florist propose to the botanist?
So she wouldn't ever leaf.

Where did the soiled garments hold their ceremony?
On the bleach.

What was the signature feature of the lawyer and attorney's reception?
The bar.

Why didn't the penguin wear a tuxedo to the wedding?
He wasn't invited.

Why did the clocks get married?
It was time.

Why did the spices get married?
It was thyme.

Why did the weekly newsmagazines get married?
It was Time.

How did the filthy carnival workers conclude their vows?
A ring toss.

Why were the chessmasters perfect for one another?

They were checkmates.

Why was the oven afraid to propose to the stove?
He didn't want to get burned.

Why were the servers so eager to get married?
They just couldn't wait any longer.

Why did the curling iron make an ideal marital counselor?
They're always able to help straighten things out.

What did the plastic surgeon wear to the reception?
A botux.

What did the groundhog get from her grandmother to wear with her dress?
Something burrowed.

Did you hear about the spider's mom who couldn't stop crying during the ceremony?
She just webbed and webbed.

How the dentist accept her vows?
She opened wide and said, "Ahhh do."

What kind of fish did the shrimp hire for the bachelor party?
Stripers.

What was the compulsive gambler's role in the wedding?
The bets man.

What did the shoe get at her bachelorette party?
Some lace.

Did you see that the barber danced with the bride?
He cut in.

WEDDINGS ARE A JOKE!

What did the entomologists feature in the middle of their reception tables?

A beautiful centipede.

What did the mattress salesmen and and the carpenter admire about each other?

Their good nail beds.

Why did the U.S. service member fall for the the woman with long limbs?

She was Army.

What did the dentist have as an appetizer at their reception?
Steak tartar.

What did the pigeons drive off in after the reception?
A coop.

How much did it cost for the fingers to get married?
Several digits.

How are the furniture designers enjoying their marriage?
Sofa so good.

What was the chicken's role at the barnyard wedding?
Fowler girl.

Why did the bass fall for the fishing hook?
It was very alluring.

Did you hear about the truck drivers that got engaged?
They're in it for the long haul.

What did the professional bowlers serve at their reception?
Turkey.

Who presided over the edamame's wedding?
The Justice of the Peas.

What did the joeys say when they got married?
"I roo."

Why did the burglar tear up as he ransacked the gift table?
He always crimes at weddings.

Did you hear about the watches who were in love?
They couldn't keep their hands off each other.

What was all the rage at the plant's reception?

The photosynthesis booth.

What did the flim flam artist get the happy couple?
A wedding grift.

What kind of weather did the tadpoles hope for at their wedding?
Froggy.

Why were the boats excited to begin their marriage?
They were ready to get hitched.

Did you hear about the English groomsman who left the wedding early after refusing to pay for his tuxedo rental?
He made a stunning Brexit.

Why did the bride think she could drop four sizes before the ceremony?

Because this is the society we've created. Isn't there something wrong with this question?

Printed in Great Britain
by Amazon